DEMI SCHNEIDER AND SCARLETT
KITCHENER

Essential Guide to Visiting Dalyan

*All You Need to Know on the Where to, What to and
How to in Dalyan, that Google and the Brochures
Don't Tell You.*

First edition

This book was professionally typeset on Reedsy.
Find out more at reedsy.com

Contents

Acknowledgments

Extending Acknowledgments to Our Turkish Family:
Ali and Sara at Tapa
Arif and Meryl
Aysu at BC Spa
Baki
Dorien and Tolga
Eddie
Ekrem
Eray
Erim
Ertugul, Ronaldo and staff at Ali's
'Harry' and staff of Kordons
Ïsa and family
Jed
Mr Turbo
Murat
Okan and his mum
Önder, Salih and staff at Brilliant Tours
Ricky and his mum
Selim at Volkan's Adventures
Staff at the Riverside restaurant
Tarkan
Tayfun
Tez

Tomas

Üstün

Volkan

Yasmin and Haluk at Yasminauthentic (lovely shop!)

Yenner, Burak and staff at Yenners

And all of the other lovely people who make our stay so special ❤

1

Introduction

My connection with Dalyan began over 30 years ago during a day-long boat trip from Marmaris on my first visit to Turkey. Something about this magical place lingered with me but it wasn't until 17 years later that I had the opportunity to return, this time with my six-year-old daughter, Scarlett. We had the best time, and Dalyan's warmth and charm made us feel completely at ease. We felt welcomed and safe, and there was never a shortage of things to do.

We went back the next year, and the year after, until Dalyan became our second home, full of cherished friends and countless beautiful memories. Over time, we've found ourselves guiding fellow travellers—sharing insider tips, offering directions, and explaining the "where to," "what to," and "how to" in Dalyan. Inspired to write this guide, our aim is to make it easier for more visitors to find heir way around and enjoy all that Dalyan has to offer.

This book isn't intended as an exhaustive directory, more of a companion to help simplify your stay, from finding the boat taxi to the beach, locating the nearest ATM or doctor, or even navigating your way to

Koycegiz market after the fabulous lake crossing.

If you've already booked your holiday this guide can be your instant turn to, or, if you've yet to book, we hope you'll be inspired to do so, with the extra assurance of the local knowledge that google and the brochures don't tell you. Dalyan really is a hidden gem filled with charm and glorious delights.

2

Planning Your Trip

Tips for Packing

Bear in mind that the local shops and mini markets can supply many of your needs, including light weight, quick dry towels that cost less than £5, or hats, general self care products and plenty of clothes should you run out, so it's safe to travel light! Sun cream is relatively expensive so it's worth bringing that.

When it comes to evening attire in Dalyan, anything goes, from casual wear to something more dressy or elegant, so you can feel free to suit yourself, whatever your style or mood, although do note that the roads are not best conducive to heels. However, if you're dining at La Boheme or the Kingfisher, a slightly more polished look is expected.

Evenings in Dalyan can be a bit cooler in May and early June, as well as during September and October, so a light cardigan or wrap is usually needed. In the height of summer— late June through August —the nights are still plenty warm enough, even at midnight.

For those magical Moonlight Trips on the lake (check out the "Trips" section), a warmer layer is recommended—it can get unexpectedly chilly out there when it gets late, even in peak season.

If you're planning on some adventurous valley treks or water-based excursions, we'd recommend switching the flip-flops for something sturdier and water-friendly. Traversing uneven, slippery stones whilst wading through water can be tricky, so a pair of jelly shoes or similarly grippy footwear will keep you steady on your feet.

When it comes to electrical needs, the Turkish plugs are two-pin and need adaptors. Hotel rooms often have limited outlets, so we've learned to pack a handy, 4 socket, short extension lead. With just one plug adapter, we're set with multiple UK sockets for the travel kettle we take, our chargers, and other essentials. It makes life much easier, so might be an idea for you too!

Mosquito Spray

We recommend you don't bother bringing any insect products from the UK (unless you have allergy needs) because they don't work against the Turkish mozzies. Most mini markets and supermarkets in Dalyan stock Sinkov or OFF, both of which help keep you clear of bites.

If you are prone to being bitten, do spray every square millimetre of yourself - even under your clothes - because the mozzies are ruthless and will happily fly up skirts and wide shorts, or bite through clothing, and you won't notice until it's too late! Even if you're not prone to being bitten, a good smothering of spray is still recommended any time you're out after 6.00 p.m. Dalyan is right on the river and it is very warm, so even with the regular mass council spraying, it's worth taking the simple precaution of using some Sinkov or OFF to save the potential itching and unsightly bumps, let alone anything worse.

Weather

While a few spots remain open year-round, Dalyan's main season runs from early May to late October.

The main season starts in May with pleasantly warm, early summer days. While daytime is generally a comfortable temperature, be ready to wrap up in a cardigan or light jacket when the evenings roll in. The sea is refreshingly cool, not the bone-chilling cold of English waters, but it still won't reach its balmy peak for a few more weeks. Some years, May can see rain showers, so it's worth coming prepared.

June, July, and August do get hot—sometimes to sizzling levels! Typically, temperatures hover around a comfortable mid-to-upper 30s (°C), but be ready for surges into the 40s. On humid days, even the locals can complain bitterly about the heat! Access to air conditioning or a pool is generally a necessity, though in extreme heat, pool water can feel more like a warm soak than a cooling dip. Escape to cooler spots, like the quaint café on the "other side" (check out the Caunos description), a breezy boat trip, or a rejuvenating spa visit. Though, as mentioned, if you're up for a moonlight cruise, keep something warmer handy as the lake can surprise you with a chill, even in the hottest months.

In September, a noticeable shift sets in. Temperatures ease, and the atmosphere grows more relaxed without the buzz of school-holiday crowds. This is prime time for many visitors, with comfortably warm days and nights that invite a light layer. October often follows suit, with plenty of sunshine for swimwear-clad afternoons, though evenings are certainly cooler.

3

Welcome to Dalyan

The Town

The delightful town centre of Dalyan is compact, with mostly a single main street lined with shops and bars, highlighted by the Mosque Square. A few side streets branch off, offering additional bars and cosy restaurants to explore. You won't find any nightclubs here; even the liveliest bars typically don't pick up until after 22.00. For those seeking a more spirited atmosphere, the area near Rumours bar at the upper end of town tends to be busier and more energetic, while the riverside restaurants at both ends of town offer a quieter, more serene vibe.

You'll find the public loos in Mosque square, as shown on our map. You need to pay cash lira for entry, the cost being 10TL (25p) per person in 2024. Some are Turkish toilets with the hole in the tray, but there are plenty of standard loos too and it's all clean and pleasant. You can also have a shower if you wish for an additional small fee

Our map outlines useful locations through the town. While it's not drawn to exact scale or intended as a detailed street guide, we hope it serves as a handy reference to help you get your bearings and locate key spots around Dalyan.

The People

The majority of locals in Dalyan are warm and friendly, honest and fair, and you'll often find them eager to assist whenever they can. Many of them speak very good English. In most restaurants, you'll encounter welcoming 'front men' whose job is to invite you in, but rest assured, they do so with a polite, easygoing manner—unlike some other destinations in Turkey. A simple, friendly "No thank you" is always respected.

The long hours the staff put in and the effort they make to create a welcoming experience deserve a smile or kind response. Over the years, we've built so many friendships here that saying goodbye to them when we leave literally takes us hours—a true testament to the bonds you can form in Dalyan, as many others have too.

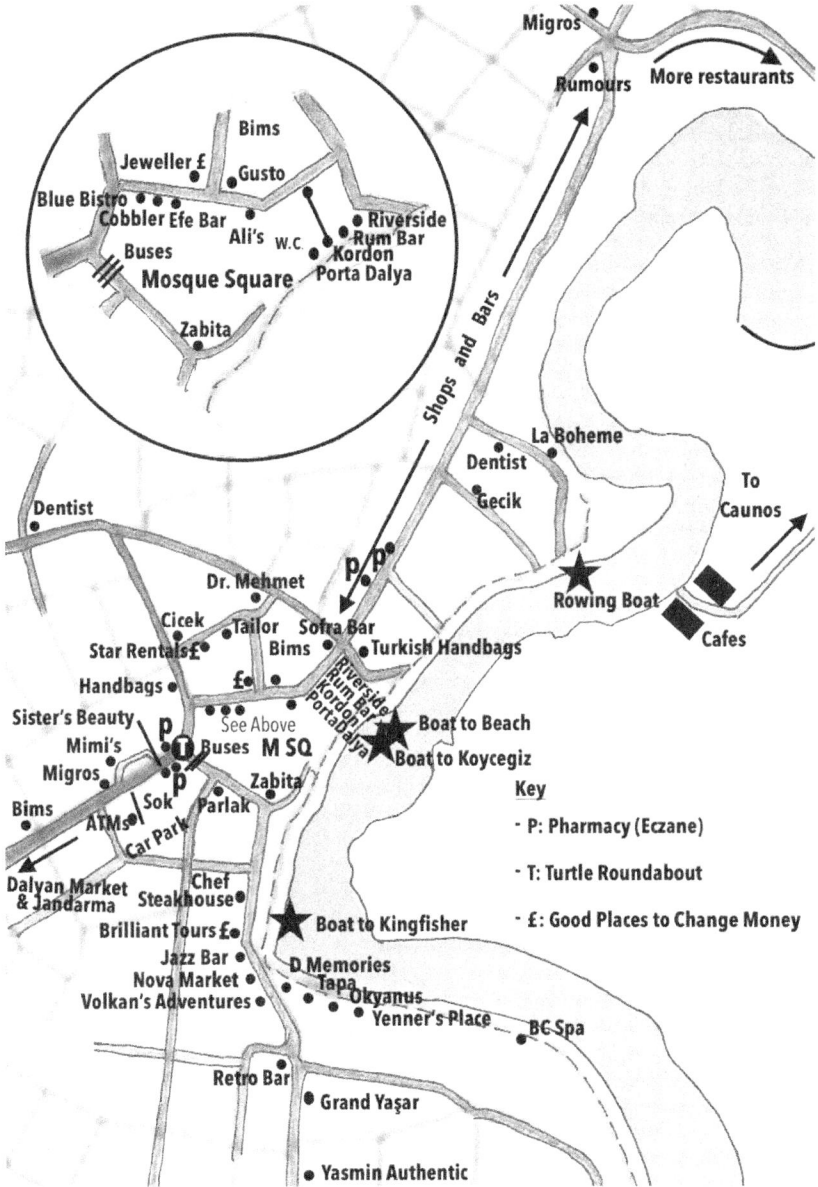

Migros

Rumours   More restaurants

Inset circle (Mosque Square area):

Bims

Jeweller £   Gusto

Blue Bistro

Cobbler Efe Bar

Ali's   W.C   Riverside   Rum Bar

Buses   Kordon

Mosque Square   Porta Dalya

Zabita

Shops and Bars

La Boheme

Dentist

Gecik

To Caunos

Dr. Mehmet

P / P

Cicek   Tailor   Sofra Bar

Star Rentals £   Bims   Turkish Handbags

Handbags   £

Sister's Beauty   Riverside Rum Bar Kordon Porta Dalya

Mimi's   P   See Above   Rowing Boat

Migros   T   Buses   M SQ   Cafes

Bims   P   Zabita   Boat to Beach

ATMs   Sok   Parlak   Boat to Koycegiz

Dalyan Market   Car Park

& Jandarma   Chef   Steakhouse

Brilliant Tours £   Boat to Kingfisher

Jazz Bar   D.Memories

Nova Market   Tapa

Volkan's Adventures   Okyanus

Yenner's Place   BC Spa

Retro Bar

Grand Yaşar

Yasmin Authentic

Dentist

Key

- P: Pharmacy (Eczane)

- T: Turtle Roundabout

- £: Good Places to Change Money

Money

The local currency is Lira and Dalyan is still very much a cash culture, albeit more places each year are accepting cards. Generally, the shops will now take cards, but drinks on boats are cash payments, as is the doctor! Be aware too that is not uncommon for hotels to charge quite large commissions on card payments, so cash can be preferable.

We would recommend taking English notes and changing them in Dalyan, which gives a much better exchange rate than in the UK. There are several places to change money, some indicated on our map, but it's worth keeping your eye open as the rates can vary from place to place and can also change frequently. We find that changing money up just for a few days ahead, or a week at most, is best.

The ATM machines are situated as shown on our map. We 100% recommend using the ING bank ATM for the best exchange rate. Also, on this machine, a huge hack to avoid paying commission is to press the button that says "Accept Without Conversion" on the left rather than "Accept With Conversion" on the right, even though is perhaps a little counter-intuitive.

The exchange rate in summer 2024 was 40TL to the pound, so 4000TL for every hundred pounds. The highest denomination note is currently 200TL, so means you are usually carrying a hefty wad of cash around! However, Dalyan is so safe and lovely, there's no need for concern. Do be warned though, that the ATM often runs out of money, or only has 50TL notes left, which makes it a laborious process getting out a decent amount of money to live on, and takes considerable time! Again, much easier to take a wad of English notes, keep them in the safe (or we keep our money in a locked suitcase) and then just change those up as you need.

Tips are almost exclusively discretionary, rather than a service charge being added to the bill. They are very welcome, especially as the local economy is very harsh. At the time of writing, Turkey has been experiencing 60% inflation, which, whilst the exchange rate soaks up much of that for British tourists, hits the locals hard.

4

Food and Drinks

Restaurants

It is said that Dalyan has more restaurant seats than hotel rooms, so you'll never be short on dining options! While finding a table is typically easy, some spots do fill up fast in late July and August, so booking ahead is a good idea—especially for favourites like La Boheme and Ali's, both shown on our map.

The culinary scene in Dalyan is a feast of flavours, offering everything from hearty meat dishes and freshly caught fish to delicious vegetarian and classic Turkish cuisine. Whilst most of the restaurants are very good, chefs can change from year to year, so sometimes a restaurant that is great one year may not be the next, and vice versa. For the best insider tips, we recommend asking on the Dalyan Visitors Facebook page about a week before your trip. If you're a foodie, it's the perfect way to learn the latest recommendations and hidden gems!

For quieter restaurants in idyllic settings, those along the river are best. From Mosque Square you can see the river path and enjoy the restaurants there on the left, or bear right, which takes you up to "D Memories", at the fork of the main road as shown on our map, and follows past Tapa, the fish restaurant, Okyanus and Yenner's Place, before the path winds along the river with more spaced out restaurants the further you walk, for a more serene and nature loving experience. A ten or fifteen minute stroll will take you past several delightful places, or keep going even further as you wish.

The top end of town, past Rumours, takes you on a path with many restaurants on both sides of the road. Those on the right have lovely tables overlooking the river and the rock tombs and are very peaceful.

There are also restaurants out of town for a change, including the very excellent Kingfisher. A new shuttle service with a boat taxi makes this experience much more accessible but also does mean it can be more crowded. This boat departs from the river more or less opposite the Brilliant Tours office. You can also book it from Grand Yasar on the left as you go up past Volkan's Adventures; you'll see it advertised on the board outside. If you want a quiet meal there, it's best to go lunch time or after 9.45 p.m.

Gluten Free

In truth, it's not so easy for those with dietary needs.

For Gluten Free food, The Turkish word is Gluteniz. You can buy Gluten Free items in Migros supermarket, but buying gluten free bread in Dalyan is not ideal; most of what is available is pretty disgusting. The Dalyano cafe (just behind Dr. Mehmet) sells reasonable gluten free bread and the A101 supermarket (just further up the road from Migros) sells gluten free crackers. We take our own gluten free bread from the UK and give it to the waiter when we're ordering.

In restaurants, do be careful with some soups as they might be thickened with flour. Do not eat börek or baklava. Be especially careful of the rice! It is usually served as rice with darker bits that are actually roasted pasta, so do make sure a restaurant can provide rice only - which is often not an option.

If you are gluten free and have booked a boat trip, we strongly advise taking your own bread and, if a beer drinker, your own gluten free beer, as these are not available on boats. Gluten free beer is available in some restaurants, and some mini markets such as the Nova market shown on our map. The mini market price is around half that charged in restaurants, understandably, and makes a cheap bar bill on a boat trip!

Water and Ice Cubes

While it's perfectly fine to use the tap water for brushing your teeth, drinking it is not a good idea; it's best to stick to bottled water, which is readily available and inexpensive. Another tip: keep an eye out for ice cubes in your drinks. If you have a sensitive stomach, it's worth asking whether the ice is made from tap or bottled water. Avoiding tap-water ice could spare you an unpleasant reaction— stomach bugs can really put a damper on a holiday! If you need a doctor, see below!

Bakers

The best Bakers shop in town is notoriously Parlak, shown on our map opposite the row of mini buses. They have gorgeous breads and pastries, although unfortunately not gluten free. There is usually a long queue of locals formed from early morning, which is always a good sign!

5

The Beach

Iztuzu Beach

This beautiful beach welcomes visitors from 8:00 a.m. to 8:00 p.m., but once the sun sets, it becomes the sanctuary for the Loggerhead Turtles (also known as Caretta Caretta turtles), who come out of the sea to lay their eggs. In the summer months, you'll see small protective cages scattered along the sand to safeguard these precious nests.

Getting to the fabulous 4.5 km stretch of Iztuzu Beach is a memorable experience in itself. You can take a scenic minibus ride to the Turtle Hospital end, or hop aboard a charming taxi-boat that brings you to the opposite end. You can return the same way, or choose a leisurely stroll from end to end— about an hour's walk that is absolutely beautiful - and return from there. Though if you're visiting during the peak heat of summer, we would definitely recommend a hat and cover-up; the midday sun between 12:00 and 15.00 can be intense! We sometimes get the first mini bus to the beach and walk to the other end to spend the day, or leave the boat end at about 16:30 and walk the length of the beach back to the minibus. It is always beautiful and so worthwhile.

For the minibus route, head to the line of mini buses just down from Turtle Roundabout, as marked on our map. The journey takes around half an hour and must be one of the most picturesque bus rides anywhere, with vistas that are arguably even more stunning on the return trip. The bus runs at least every half-hour starting from 9:30 a.m. and is a very budget-friendly option. This end of the beach is popular with locals as it allows for car access.

If you would prefer to get the boat taxi along the river, there are several boat owners who will offer to take you to the beach as you walk down the river path, but we recommend getting the public taxi boat from the point further down, as shown on our map, by the Rum Bar. While prices have increased substantially in recent years (£6.25 return per adult in 2024), it still offers very good value. The 40-minute ride each way is an enchanting journey. You'll pass Dalyan's famed rock tombs and weave through tall reeds with the beautiful mountains all around—a truly unforgettable introduction to the beach. Boats depart from 9:30 throughout the summer, though departure times are very flexible, depending on when the boat fills. We choose to find this unpredictability part of the Turkish charm! In September, boats run a bit later, still following the same "full boat" ethos. .

Once at the beach, you'll find golden sands, enticing sea and the option of sunbeds and umbrellas. In 2024, these could be rented for a daily fee of £7 for two beds and an umbrella, paid in cash to a friendly attendant who comes to you once you've settled in. In front of the sunbeds, a wide section is roped off to protect any turtle nests, so no sitting or sunbathing is allowed on this strip. If you don't want to hire a sunbed or if you prefer to set up closer to the water, just pick a spot the other side of the rope. The tide is gentle so you can comfortably enjoy the sun and sea, although do note that no parasols or deck chairs are allowed.

Each end of the beach offers changing huts and toilets for your convenience. Both ends of the beach also have rustic shacks, offering hot and cold food, ice creams, and drinks (non-alcoholic). While prices on some items like crisps may seem steep, most other options are reasonable. For budget-friendly snacks, consider picking them up in town before you go!

If you arrive at the boat taxi end, there are two paths onto the beach that fork to the left and the right respectively. If you take the right hand path, we recommend choosing a sunbed or picking a spot in front the rope, a good distance either side of the wooden path as it goes down to the sea. Between 12.00 and 14.00 that path gets very busy with a constant stream of tour groups arriving for a dip in the sea. Pitching your space a few metres either side ensures more personal space and peace.

The shallow waters make it a great spot for children and non-swimmers to splash around, but keep an eye out! When the wind picks up in the afternoons, the waves can become quite powerful—great for some zealous wave jumping but occasionally strong enough to merit caution. Just sitting at the water's edge and letting the warm waves wash over you can be a delight.

The Turtle Hospital is a poignant part of Dalyan's history, thanks to the inspiring work of the indomitable "Captain June." She fell in love with Iztuzu Beach and the Caretta Caretta turtles and led a fierce campaign to protect it from the plans for a massive 5-star hotel. Thanks to her efforts, the beach was declared a protected natural area. Captain June founded the Sea Turtle Conservation Foundation for future protection and was a passionate environmental advocate until her passing in 2022. You can still see the hut where she lived near the Turtle Hospital—a humble tribute to a truly remarkable woman.

6

Places of Interest

Caunos

If you are remotely into history or ancient ruins, Caunos is a 'must-see'. The ruins themselves are spectacular. It's not quite Ephesus or Patara, yet there is lots to see, spread over a wide area, and has an almost complete amphitheatre. We would recommend allowing around 60 - 90 minutes for your time there. There is lots of see and there are information boards dotted across the site. There is no shade to speak of, so in summer months, it's best to go early morning.

There are boat trips that stop off there, but it's still a 10 - 15 minute walk from where they dock. Alternatively, you can go by yourself, first crossing the river and then either walking the 1.5 km path, or getting the tractor, although we've found the tractor very elusive. To get across the river, head to the point marked on our map and wait for a lady in a tiny rowing boat to come and get you! It's a small fee of about £1.25 return (in 2024) per person. The rowing boat service starts at 8.30 a.m.

Over the other side there are 2 little cafes; we would highly recommend the one on the right. The ladies are lovely, but they don't speak any English. You can sit at a table or in one of the very comfortable cushioned seating areas. It's great to come here for breakfast or lunch or just a drink and relax, regardless of going to Caunos! We often do, although, if you're gluten free, we recommend taking your own bread, or flour for crepes/pancakes if you want something other than chips.

If you need some help finding the Caunos path, the lovely ladies will point you in the right direction. Along the way, you'll pass a few stalls with the home-occupants selling honey, olive oil and knitted items. If you can, do buy something - it's a long day sat there just to sell a few things to make ends meet.

Having finally got to Caunos, a steepish, very rough path takes you up to the entrance. It is open from 8.30 - 19.30 in summer and 17.30 in winter. It's really cheap to get in - about £2 per person in 2024. There's a small shaded area with a few tables and chairs, with a fridge to purchase a cold drink but nothing more. There are some toilets further down the path, as signposted.

There are wooden structures to walk on in parts, though also some of the original stone steps and ground, so is not at all suitable for those with walking difficulties.

On your return, you can enjoy the oasis of the cafe before getting the rowing boat back.

Markets

If you love markets, you're in for a treat! Turkey is renowned for its vibrant, bustling markets and Dalyan and the surrounding areas offer plenty of opportunities to soak in the sights, sounds, and scents of an authentic Turkish market experience.

Dalyan Market

Every Saturday morning Dalyan hosts its own market, a 10-15 minute walk out of the town. From Turtle Roundabout, head towards Migros, carry on past the red petrol station and at the fork, follow the road to the right. As you pass the tourism school on your left, turn left, and you'll find it 100 metres up on your left. It offers an array of goods, making it fun to explore, yet is comparatively expensive, being in a tourist area. Some bartering is definitely an option.

Koycegiz Market

Every Monday, a 75 minute boat trip across the breathtaking, beautiful lake takes you to the two thriving markets found in the scenic town of Koycegiz.

Numerous operators along the river path will vie for your business, or you can opt for the government-run public boat, indicated on our map. This offers the lowest price and the longest duration, leaving at 10:30 and returning around 16:15. Some operators offer slightly superior boats, at a higher price. Some operators also offer detours to mud baths or hot springs, so double-check their itinerary based on your preferences.

On arriving at Kocegiz, it really helps to know where the markets are because invariably the boat captains don't speak much English, or don't tell you, and they're not obvious from the harbour. It is a little bit of a stroll, especially if the weather is very hot, but well worth it. With the lake on your left, bear right and you'll easily see the bottom of the High Street.

If you need the public toilets, first keep left and then bear right and you'll see them on the left, with a lovely lady sat ready to take your liras to enter. She crochets whilst sat there and produces the most stunningly beautiful items. She doesn't speak English but it's amazing how gestures and facial expressions can speak volumes!

Otherwise, having found the bottom of the High Street, keep walking up there on the left, past the shops, the supermarket, the bakers and jewellers, until you eventually get to the "Alcohol House" corner shop and a man selling watermelons. The market is there on your left with a few stalls on the road that lead you into the main section which offers a huge array of fruit, vegetables, olives, cheese and nuts, along with clothes, bedding, shoes, household items and lots more, at great prices. A reel of good quality cotton and suchlike costs pennies compared to England, so can be well worth a purchase. Being more for locals, we'd encourage generosity over bartering; a small saving for us is a meaningful amount to the vendors.

On exiting, cross the road and and walk back down the other side of the High Street. On your left there's another market, not so big and with no food stuffs, but still plenty of wares of all sorts. We find this market a bit more pricey than the top one, though there are still some great purchases to be had if you wish.

Be sure to return to your boat in good time; the captains have strict mooring times so leave promptly. It's a long bus journey or expensive taxi ride if you miss it.

Ortaca market

As a third option, there's Ortaca market on a Friday. Frequent minibuses can be found just down from Turtle Roundabout as shown on our map. The pleasant journey takes about half an hour and the bus actually turns into the station at Ortaca to easily know you're at the right point to get off. Just follow everyone else making a beeline for the main street, turn right and the market is just down on the right. Prices tend to be much lower here than in Dalyan as the market caters more to locals, so again we'd encourage generosity over bartering.

Ortaca itself is a lively little town. After browsing the market, you can choose to take a leisurely stroll along its streets and pop into the clothing shops and jewellers that also offer air-conditioned respite! Shops line the streets near the market and around the bus station, as well as back up on the main bus route.

Day Trips

There are a wide range of other trips available, from various excellent boat excursions and jeep safaris, to horse riding and exploration of other historic ruins and more. These can be booked through numerous companies scattered throughout the town. Most have boards outside detailing what they offer, and often brochures for you to take away too. It's worth taking the time to shop around, not only for the price, but to ensure you find the trip that best suits your preferences and expectations.

One of our favourites is the 12 Islands Tour. This adventure begins with a mini-bus ride to the picturesque Mega Yacht Marina in charming Gocek. From there, you'll board a boat and set sail through stunning turquoise bays, stopping for swims in warm (seasonally!), clear waters and enjoying lunch on board. We find it the perfect way to feel away from it all and completely unwind.

The 12 Islands Tour is widely available but offers varied experiences based on what you choose. The more budget-friendly options typically involve larger boats with many passengers. For a more intimate experience, there are also smaller, select gullets available. Be sure to check what kind of shade coverage the boat offers if you'd prefer not to spend the day in direct sunlight.

For us, Volkan's Adventures has become our go-to. While it is a little more expensive, we feel it's worth every penny. With a maximum of 18 people on a luxury boat designed to hold 35, it guarantees a comfortable journey, exceptional food, plenty of shade, and an overall superior experience. When the charismatic Volkan himself is the tour guide on his 12 Islands Tour or one of his many exclusive trips, it certainly is an adventure!

Another highlight is the Moonlight Tour, which we think is simply magical—especially on Volkan's boats. Due to Jandarma regulations, boats must now return by 23.00. which means missing out on the full darkness after midnight, but the stars are still breathtaking. We recommend downloading the Sky Guide app on iOS; it reveals exactly what you're gazing at—the Milky Way, Zodiac constellations, planets— and you'll spot plenty of satellites too!

7

Shops

While Dalyan doesn't boast the extensive shopping options found in Kusadasi, Fethiye, or Antalya for leather goods and fashion, you'll find a few "genuine fake" bag shops, a genuine Turkish bag shop, quality jewellers, and an array of clothing, lamps and souvenirs as you walk around the town, particularly on the stretch up towards Rumours Bar.

There is also a line of little stalls set up each evening near Mosque Square with locals selling trinkets and handmade items that gives a lovely atmosphere as you walk through this part and offers some really authentic purchase opportunities.

For the more practical shops; some that we find the most useful are:

Dressmaker/Tailor

For sewing needs or custom-made outfits, the highly skilled Arif and Meryl are located just past Dr. Mehmet's office, on the left. You'll spot their shop a short distance up, easily identifiable by the clothing displayed outside. They speak very little English, but Google Translate can come in handy for more complex requests, whilst simple tasks can often be conveyed with gestures. They also have clothing for sale. Don't be put off if any of their large dogs come to greet you; they're all as soft as marshmallows!

Cobbler

If you need shoe repairs, the friendly cobbler is situated between Blue Bistro and Efe Bar—just up from Ali's restaurant and is highly recommended. His work is excellent and very affordable. He also sells shoes.

Rental

There are several places to hire electric scooter tricycles (also known as tuktuk's), e-bikes and cars in Dalyan. We use Star Rentals, shown on our map, with lovely Ricky (who also rents villas and changes money). The cost of hire is around £17-£20 per day, or £15 per day if renting over a longer period. You will need to take a driving licence in order to hire them.

Beauty and Massage

Dalyan offers plenty of options to pamper yourself, a few of which are:

- The BC Spa, which has a salt room, sauna, steam room, relaxation room, beauty rooms, and a lovely Hammam room where you can do your own Turkish bath scrub and rinse, or you can book a professional treatment to enjoy a traditional Turkish bath scrub, massages and a full range of services. Be aware that staff quality and availability can vary each year. In 2024, the use of spa facilities was £25 per person with no time limit, though booking a treatment includes spa access for free!

- Mimi's, near Migros, offers great value for manicures and pedicures. If you book a massage, they'll whisk you away in a tuk-tuk to a separate hotel location and bring you back afterward
- Sister's Beauty near Turtle Roundabout specialises in gel nails and pedicures. Though a bit pricier than other spots for pedicures, they offer a higher level of treatment.
- There's also a new nail salon, Pelin'in Güzellik Evi, midway up the High Street on the left between the two pharmacies that is quickly gaining a reputation for nails and intricate nail art.

For a more basic, yet high-quality experience, we enjoy treatments in The Dalyan Hammam, further out of town. Their services are excellent and very budget-friendly—a 60-minute massage costing just £30 in 2024. Even better, they'll pick you up from your hotel or chosen location and drop you off after your session, making it extremely convenient! It's not the spa experience of other places Dalyan has offer, but the wonderful massages most certainly compensate for this. They're contactable on +90 555 688 6771

Supermarkets

Dalyan has a range of supermarkets and mini markets, so there is plenty of opportunity to shop around to get the best of all worlds!

As shown on our map, Migros can be found just up from Turtle roundabout, and also at the top end of town near Rumours; Bims can be found in town near the tailor and further up the road from Turtle Roundabout on the right, past Migros; A101 can be found further up that road on the left, and Sok can be found near the ATMs.

As with supermarkets in the UK, they all have their pros and cons. In our experience we've found that Bims is the cheapest, Migros is best for groceries and has the best overall range, and Sok is best for beauty products. You can only get gluten free food in Migros, at the time of writing this. Also, Migros has a card, a bit like a Tesco Clubcard, which means items are often significantly cheaper at the till. Just ask for one at the checkout. The downside is they now only last for a month and then get renewed, which is horrific plastic waste for the planet! We paid £1 for ours originally many years ago but haven't paid any more since. If you do get charged it will be worth it for the saving.

There are also plenty of mini markets dotted around; no doubt you'll find your favourite.

8

Health

Pharmacies

Dalyan has four pharmacies, two located near each other on the High Street and two others on either side of Turtle Roundabout, as indicated with a P on our map. The word for Pharmacy is Eczane (pronounced edg-zarn-eh) All four are open during the day, with one operating till late at night on a rotating schedule. While we've tried to unravel the mystery of this nighttime rota, we've not been successful so far, so it's just a question of plodding round till you find the one that's open! One certainly will be, and you'll be able to obtain medication, advice, and assistance. They speak English and are very helpful.

Doctor

If you need a doctor, you can find Dr. Mehmet where indicated on our map. He is excellent and wonderfully committed and caring. You'll likely find him sitting in the entry lounge, reading his paper or maybe watching some TV, which he'll immediately cease to tend to you. You can call him on +90 532 292 2671. He is usually there till around 7.00. Or if you need, give him a ring and he will tell you hen he'll be there. He also speaks reasonable English - just speak slowly to him. And he'll come out to visit you if needs be. It's real, old-fashioned, feel good service! In 2024, a consultation was £50.

There are two additional doctors in Dalyan: one next to the Sok supermarket and another on Ataturk Bulvari just past the Montana Hotel. We have no personal experience of these. We have heard that "Jet Doctor", on the way into Dalyan (near Ada Teknik), is very expensive, but again have no personal experience.

Dentist

We now don't have a dentist in England and just come to Dalyan. We go to the one situated on the Beach Road, indicated on our map. We find the difference in service and treatment to that in the UK is beyond amazing, albeit sadly the locals struggle to afford the prices that seem so comparatively cheap to us. You can just walk in and will likely be seen within a few minutes.

The Dalyan Dentist is just off the High Street, as shown on our map, on the right before La Boheme restaurant on the left. They have a 5* rating too and offer a whole range of services.

Hospital

On the off-chance that you need to go to hospital, fear not! Yucelen Hospital is excellent.

Situated in Ortaca, about 10 km away, it only takes about 15/20 minutes to get there, with a very reasonable taxi fare of about £7.50 each way in 2024. You'll need the "Foreign Patients" department, where an interpreter will be despatched to assist you all the way.

We had a consultation, 2 MRI scans, a follow up consultation and a PRP spinal injection treatment for a slipped disc all in 2 days! And because the op day for Scarlett fell on Demi's birthday, whilst we were in the recovery room, the door opened and in came the fantastic doctor, the fabulous interpreter and a trio of nurses, armed with a gorgeous cake with candles, all singing Happy Birthday! A photo shoot ensued with an upbeat exchange of airdrops to each other!

Their wall is decorated with cards eulogising gratitude and compliments and we are not surprised. If you end up here, you'll be fine.

Police

In the unlikely event you'll need them, the local police are called the Zabita (pronounced Zabeeta) and their office is by the taxi rank near the river, as shown on our map. Some of them do speak some English. Feel free to complain if you find the music too loud or need something sorted!

Even more unlikely, for something serious, you'd need the Jandarma. They don't speak English so you'd need to use Google Translate. Their big station is a taxi ride from the centre. Sometimes they can be seen in the town. We mention all this because they exist, not because you're likely to have any trouble. They look scary, but if you're in trouble, they are lovely.

9

Conclusion

We do hope this has been an enjoyable and useful read and wish you a fabulous holiday. Many people return to Dalyan multiple times, even those who 'never go to the same place twice', and many end up like us, totally hooked! We hope you enjoy the charm and beauty and delights that Dalyan has to offer and leave with lots of cherished memories.

If you have found this book helpful, we'd be really appreciative if you could please leave us a favourable review on Amazon - it would mean a lot to us. Thank you.

About the Author

We have been going to Dalyan for the past 15 years, spending more and more time there each year. We've met the most amazing people, forged unforgettable friendships, have a treasure trove of cherished memories, and can't wait to go back each time.

Our love of this place has inspired us to write this guide to help others enjoy Dalyan too!

Printed in Dunstable, United Kingdom